ISBN 978-1-333-42136-6
PIBN 10502382

Author: Pepper, George H. (George Hubba),

Title: Stone effigy pipe from Kentucky, t

Year: 1920

Publications of the Museum of the American Indian, Heye Foundation

THE GEORGE G. HEYE EXPEDITION
CONTRIBUTIONS TO SOUTH AMERICAN ARCHAEOLOGY
Vol. 1
The Antiquities of Manabi, Ecuador: A Preliminary Report. By Marshall H. Saville. 1907. $25.00.
Vol. 2
The Antiquities of Manabi, Ecuador: Final Report. By Marshall H. Saville. 1910. $25.00.

CONTRIBUTIONS FROM THE MUSEUM OF THE AMERICAN INDIAN, HEYE FOUNDATION
Vol. 1
No. 1: Lucayan Artifacts from the Bahamas. By Theodoor de Booy. Reprinted from *Amer. Anthropol.*, Vol. 15, 1913, No. 1. 50c.

No. 2: Precolumbian Decoration of the Teeth in Ecuador, with some Account of the Occurrence of the Custom in other parts of North and South America. By Marshall H. Saville. Reprinted from *Amer. Anthropol.*, Vol. 15, 1913, No. 3. 50c.

No. 3: Certain Kitchen-middens in Jamaica. By Theodoor de Booy. Reprinted from *Amer. Anthropol.*, Vol. 15, 1913, No. 3. (*Reprinted, 1919.*) 50c.

No. 4: Porto Rican Elbow-stones in the Heye Museum, with discussion of similar objects elsewhere. By J. Walter Fewkes. Reprinted from *Amer Anthropol.*, Vol. 15, 1913, No. 3. 50c.

INDIAN NOTES
AND MONOGRAPHS

VOL. X   No. 4

A SERIES OF PUBLICA-
TIONS RELATING TO THE
AMERICAN ABORIGINES

OLD SAUK AND FOX BEADED GARTERS

BY
M. R. HARRINGTON

NEW YORK
MUSEUM OF THE AMERICAN INDIAN
HEYE FOUNDATION
1920

This series of INDIAN NOTES AND MONO-
GRAPHS is devoted primarily to the publica-
tion of the results of studies by members of
the staff of the Museum of the American
Indian, Heye Foundation, and is uniform
with HISPANIC NOTES AND MONOGRAPHS,
published by the Hispanic Society of
America, with which organization this
Museum is in cordial coöperation.

Title: Archaic Iowa tomahawk / by M. R.

OLD SAUK AND
FOX BEADED GARTERS

BY

M. R. HARRINGTON

Author: Harrington, M. R. (Mark Raymond),

Title: Archaic Iowa tomahawk / by M. R.

Year: 1920

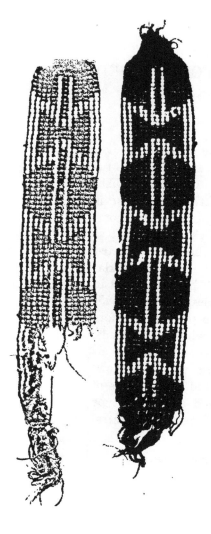

HARRINGTON—BEADED GARTERS

SAUK AND FOX BEADED GARTERS

OLD SAUK AND FOX BEADED GARTERS

By M. R. HARRINGTON

F ALL the hundreds of Indian woven bead garters in the Museum of the American Indian, Heye Foundation, the oldest is probably a pair, represented in the accompanying illustration, which formed part of the contents of a "war-bundle" collected from the Sauk and Fox Indians of Oklahoma. As the bird-quill belt described in another paper (this series, vol. x, no. 5) may be said to belong to the period before the Indians obtained the white man's beads, this pair of garters may be regarded as representing the period immediately following, for the large blue and white beads of which they are composed are of the type brought among the Indians in the central districts west of the Mississippi by the first white traders, usually called "pony traders" by the Indians because they brought their stocks of trade goods on pack-ponies. A little later, when smaller beads like those in present use were brought in, the "pony-trader beads" soon fell from favor in this district, and are seen only on the older pieces of Indian handiwork, although in the Northwest they seem to have lingered longer.

The garters referred to are decidedly the worse for age and wear, but the more perfect of the two still measures $2\frac{1}{8}$ in. wide by 11 in. long, and was once undoubtedly longer. The two are made on a yellowish brown native yarn, probably buffalo-wool, which, unlike more modern bead garters, was woven out at the ends fully an inch beyond the beadwork, beyond which the yarn evidently hung loose as a fringe, in this respect resembling the recent specimens of this class.

The design consists of three hourglass-shaped figures outlined with a double row of white beads on a blue ground, and connected by two rows of white beads with a blue row between, extending down the center of the garter.

The writer does not remember having seen any other example of solid beadwork belonging to this period, although we have in the collection a few woven buffalo-wool armbands, necklaces, and sashes, which show a few "pony-trader beads" strung on the yarn and woven in so as to form a pattern. These are all from Sauk and Fox and Osage war-bundles.

These garters and the bundle of which they formed a part are mentioned in the writer's book on "Sacred Bundles of the Sac and Fox Indians," *Anthr. Publ. University of Pennsylvania Museum*, vol. IV, no. 2, p. 201, Phila., 1914.

Author: Pepper, George H. (George Hubb

Title: Wooden image from Kentucky, by

Year: 1921

CPSIA information can be obtained
at www.ICGtesting.com
Printed in the USA
BVHW090319211118
533509BV00032BA/4934/P